Blessings,
Beth Fore

Whispers in the Wind, Shouts in the Storm!

Anna Beth Fore

CROSSBOOKS

CrossBooks™
A Division of LifeWay
1663 Liberty Drive
Bloomington, IN 47403
www.crossbooks.com
Phone: 1-866-879-0502

© 2013 Anna Beth Fore. All rights reserved.

No part of this book may be reproduced, stored in a retrieval system, or transmitted by any means without the written permission of the author.

Scriptures taken from the Holy Bible, New International Version®, NIV®. Copyright © 1973, 1978, 1984, 2011 by Biblica, Inc.™ Used by permission of Zondervan. All rights reserved worldwide. www.zondervan.com The "NIV" and "New International Version" are trademarks registered in the United States Patent and Trademark Office by Biblica, Inc.™
All rights reserved.

First published by CrossBooks 03/08/2013

Library of Congress Control Number: 2013903103

ISBN: 978-1-4627-2542-7 (sc)
ISBN: 978-1-4627-2543-4 (e)
ISBN: 978-1-4627-2544-1 (hc)

Library of Congress Control Number: Applied For

Printed in the United States of America

This book is printed on acid-free paper.

Any people depicted in stock imagery provided by Thinkstock are models, and such images are being used for illustrative purposes only.

Certain stock imagery © Thinkstock.

Because of the dynamic nature of the Internet, any web addresses or links contained in this book may have changed since publication and may no longer be valid. The views expressed in this work are solely those of the author and do not necessarily reflect the views of the publisher, and the publisher hereby disclaims any responsibility for them.

Contents

1. Whispers in the Wind 1

2. Your Creation, Lord 17

3. Relationships 45

4. Jesus 65

5. God's Holy Spirit 93

6. Shouts in the Storm 107

7. Hope 145

I dedicate this book
to the Lord of my life
and
to my parents,
David LeRoy and Eloise Thompson,
who introduced me to Him
and served Him faithfully.

Acknowledgments

My family has been listening to my poems for decades, and I appreciate their patience, kind words, and encouragement throughout the years. I am especially grateful to my sister, Judy, who has always encouraged and supported me in every thing I do. As a public school teacher for thirty-four years, I wrote many poems for my students and for my faculty and friends. They were very gracious to listen to my poems, and I appreciate their kind words and encouragement.

I have been a Bible teacher for several years and have included some of my poems in the lessons I've shared with other women. These women have really encouraged and inspired me to continue writing poetry. It is because of their encouraging words that I have finally completed this book, so I am forever grateful to them.

There are several women who read different versions of this book and gave me their honest opinions and suggestions: Rhesa Higgins, Marilyn Coody, Mae Green, and Mary Ann Robinson. I am especially thankful to them for their time, their encouragement, and their willingness to be honest and open with me. As a result, the final copy of this book is very different from the rough draft, and I am pleased with the final version. Thank you, ladies!

My parents always encouraged me in my writing, and though they have gone to be with the Lord, they made it financially possible for me to publish this book. It is my hope and prayer that they would be pleased with the final result.

Finally, I am so thankful that God has given me the love of writing poetry and that He has allowed me to enjoy this outlet for expressing myself since I was a child. This book is intended to offer up praise and honor to my heavenly Father.

Whispers in the Wind, Shouts in the Storm!

Sometimes I whisper my thoughts and questions and prayers to God in the wind. Natural and supernatural wonders can be observed daily in God's creation. New truths and understandings are revealed every day as people open their minds and hearts to God's revelations. God's presence can be seen, heard and felt in nature, in people, in His Word and in people's spirits.

I enjoy expressing my thoughts in poetry, so I have written many poems over the years. Some of these poems are "whispers in the wind". These are poems and prayers that are written in times of praise and thanksgiving, reflectiveness and meditation. There are days when life is calm and peaceful and there is time to commune and worship God in the stillness and quiet and to whisper words of thankfulness and gratitude for His presence and His blessings.

Other poems have been written as a result of the difficult circumstances in life. These are "shouts in the storm". There are circumstances and events that happen that human beings don't understand and don't like. There are many questions that people would like to have answered, especially about the pain and trials that they, or someone they know, must bear.

There are days when people feel disconnected and distant from God. Sometimes they wonder where He is and why He isn't answering their prayers and pleas in the midst of the difficult storms of life that they face. People need His presence, His peace and His comfort more than ever in these times of loneliness and despair.

Christians know that they can talk with God any time, regardless of the circumstances. As a Christian, I find peace and comfort in expressing these thoughts in poetry, so I have written these poems as "shouts in the storm".

Perhaps you have whispered some of these same prayers in the wind and shouted some of these same cries in the storm. As fellow travelers on the pathway of life, we share many common experiences. Hopefully, you will relate to *Whispers in the Wind, Shouts in the Storm!* in a way that will draw you into a more intimate relationship with Almighty God.

*Whispers in the Wind,
Shouts in the Storm!*

†

Then they cried out to the Lord
in their trouble, and he brought them
out of their distress. He stilled the storm
to a whisper; the waves of the sea were hushed.
They were glad when it grew calm,
and he guided them to their desired haven.
(Psalm 107:28–30)

Whispers in the Wind, Shouts in the Storm!

*Sometimes life is simple and easy,
and I whisper to You in the wind.
I offer You praise and thanksgiving
for all of the blessings You send.*

*Sometimes the days are sunny,
and there is beauty everywhere.
I honor You with a grateful heart
and thank You for being there.*

*Sometimes life is difficult and messy,
and nothing makes sense to me.
I shout and groan in the storm
and beg You to hear my plea.*

*Sometimes life really hurts, Lord,
and it is filled with heartache and pain.
I pour out my soul to You for relief,
pleading that my prayer not be in vain.*

*Sometimes I shout to You in the storm,
and sometimes I whisper in the wind,
but whether I shout or whisper, Lord,
I feel Your presence with me as my friend.*

1

Whispers in the Wind

In the morning, O Lord, you hear
my voice; in the morning I lay my requests
before you and wait in expectation.
(Psalm 5:3)

Whispers at Dawn

I sit quietly in the still of the morning
at the dawn of a brand-new day.
I hear Your voice in Your Holy Word,
and I whisper to You as I pray.

I praise Your name for who You are,
and I extol You in awe and thanksgiving.
I honor You with my worship in words
and shout hallelujahs as I sing.

I whisper Your name in the morning,
and it brings me great joy and peace.
I whisper Your name as I wait on You
to carry my burdens and give me release.

I commune with You each morning
and ask for Your guidance and lead.
I seek Your will through Your Spirit,
who gives me strength for my every need.

I seek to trust You more each day
and place each moment in Your hands.
I ask You to remind me of Your faithfulness
as I behold Your footprints in the sand.

I whisper my prayers to You at dawn,
and You remind me that I am free.
I whisper Your name in adoration,
and You give me peace and serenity.

Anna Beth Fore

Now faith is being sure
of what we hope for
and certain of what we do not see.
(Hebrews 11:1)

Faith in You, God

*Faith is reaching upward
when You extend Your hand to me.
Faith is trusting in You
to give me peace and security.
When I feel lost and alone,
faith is knowing that You love me so much.
When I am fearful and full of doubt,
You are near, and I feel Your comforting touch.
Faith is the light that guides my feet
when the world is full of sin.
Faith gives me optimism and hope
as Christ's blood makes me holy within.
Faith is the assurance of things hoped for
and the evidence of things I do not see.
Faith is the guarantee of an inheritance,
of a home with You for eternity.*

Anna Beth Fore

I will praise you with the harp
for your faithfulness, O my God;
I will sing praise to you with the lyre,
O Holy One of Israel. My lips will
shout for joy when I sing praise to you—
I, whom you have redeemed.
(Psalm 71:22–23)

Praises to My Father

I call out Your name, dear Father,
for You alone are righteous and holy.
I praise and honor and glorify Your name,
for You alone are sovereign and worthy.

I lift up my voice in songs of praise,
and to You alone my blessings bring.
I bow before You in awe and adoration
for You, Jehovah God, are my exalted King.

You are my Creator and Sustainer,
and I long to see Your face.
You are my Savior and Redeemer,
and I am saved by Your amazing grace.

I lift up my eyes to the heavens,
and I marvel at the wonders I see.
I hear the mighty roar of the ocean,
and I stand in awe of Your majesty.

Father, You alone are my master,
and You alone have the power to save.
You alone sacrificed Your Son for me
and resurrected Your Son from the grave.

I offer my heart only to You, Lord,
and I thank You for saving my soul.
Thank You for putting my broken pieces
back together and making me whole.

Anna Beth Fore

Each of the four living creatures
had six wings and was covered with eyes
all around, even under his wings.
Day and night they never stop saying:
"Holy, holy, holy is the Lord God Almighty,
who was, and is, and is to come."
(Revelation 4:8)

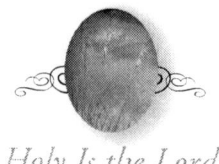

Holy Is the Lord

Holy, holy, holy
are You, Lord Almighty.
You alone are worthy
to be praised by me.

You are the great I Am
from whom all blessings flow.
You are Jehovah God,
in prayer to You I go.

You alone are worthy
of all honor and praise.
Someday I'll see Your face
and on Your glory gaze.

Worthy are You, the Lamb,
for You alone were slain.
Worthy are You, my God,
for You alone will reign.

Holy, holy, holy
are You, the God of majesty.
You will rule Your kingdom
for all eternity.

Anna Beth Fore

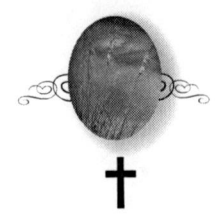

But he said to me, "My grace
is sufficient for you, for my power
is made perfect in weakness."
Therefore I will boast all the more
gladly about my weaknesses, so that
Christ's power may rest on me.
(2 Corinthians 12:9-10)

Give Me Your Grace

Today I fall down on my knees
and bow my head and face.
Today I pray that You hear my pleas,
give me an extra portion of Your grace.

I've tried to be still and wait patiently
for You to answer my prayer.
I've tried to open my eyes to see
that in the quietness You are still there.

I do not know the plans You have for me,
but I want to hear what You say.
I want to surrender my life completely,
and You alone will I trust and obey.

Please give me comfort and peace
as I seek to follow Your lead.
Please help this inward strife to cease
and to know that Your plans will succeed.

Lord, help me to give up everything
and in assurance truly believe.
When I am the sacrifice I bring,
Your blessings I will receive.

Anna Beth Fore

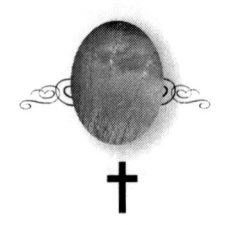

Because of the Lord's great love
we are not consumed, for his compassions
never fail. They are new every morning;
great is your faithfulness.
(Lamentations 3:22–23)

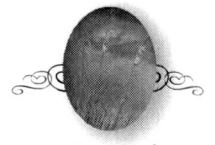

Today Is a Brand-New Day

Today is a brand-new day, Father,
filled with hope and opportunities.
Help me submit and follow Your lead
by beginning this day on my knees.

You have a plan for my life, Father,
I don't know the direction it will take,
but I pray for faith and obedience
to follow You and never forsake.

Help me look at each person I meet
as a special creation from You.
Open my heart and eyes, Father,
help me see from Your point of view.

Help me listen to other people, Father,
and hear what they have to say.
Help me minister to their needs, Lord,
and offer them hope for today.

Help me rejoice in today, Father,
with no anxiety about tomorrow.
Help me live for You in this moment
and forget about yesterday's sorrow.

Take my hand and lead me, Father,
help me walk in the light of Your way.
Cover me with Your new mercies,
for today is a brand-new day.

Anna Beth Fore

Trust in the Lord with all your heart
and lean not on your own understanding;
in all your ways acknowledge him,
and he will make your paths straight.
(Proverbs 3:5-6)

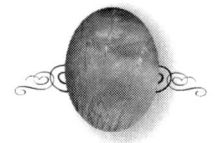

May I Completely Trust in You, Lord

*May I trust in You, Lord, with all of my heart,
in my inner self, with all of my being.
Help me live a sacrificial life of faithfulness,
to honor You with steadfastness and believing.*

*May I cast all of my burdens and cares on You, Lord,
and leave my worries and anxieties behind.
Help me to depend on You in every situation,
and give You control of my heart and mind.*

*May I lean not on my own understanding, Lord,
when my thinking shows weakness and flaw.
Help me obey Your wisdom, rather than mine,
and to submit to Your will in praise and awe!*

*May I confess my complete helplessness, Lord,
and plead for Your daily mercies and grace.
Help me to be changed into the likeness of Christ
so that His reflection will be seen in my face.*

*May I surrender all of my control to You, Lord,
so that You can mold me into what You want me to be.
Help me not to resist Your will in favor of mine,
so that others will praise You through my humility.*

*May I trust in You, Lord, with all of my heart,
and offer every part of my being to You.
Help me live a life of faith and obedience,
in every breath and every thing that I do.*

Anna Beth Fore

2

Your Creation, Lord

In the beginning
God created the heavens and the earth.
(Genesis 1:1)

God saw all that he had made,
and it was very good. And
there was evening, and there
was morning—the sixth day.
(Genesis 1:31)

Your Creation, Lord

Your Creation, God

In the beginning, God, You were there,
but the earth was formless and darkness was everywhere.
On day one, You created the light,
and You called it day and the darkness You called night.
On day two, You created the sky,
separating it from the waters below and placing it up high.
On day three, You created the land and the seas,
and on the land You created plants with seeds and fruit-bearing trees.
On day four, You created the sun, moon, and stars for this reason:
to give light to the earth and to mark the days, years, and seasons.
On day five, God, You created the birds of the air
and the creatures in the sea.
You blessed them and commanded them to increase abundantly.
On day six, You created the land animals, man and woman,
and You said that it was good.
You gave the people power over the living things to serve them as food.
On day seven, You rested, once the heavens and earth were complete.
You blessed the day and made it holy, after finishing this miraculous feat.

Anna Beth Fore

For since the creation of the world
God's invisible qualities—
his eternal power and divine nature—
have been clearly seen,
being understood from what has been made,
so that men are without excuse.
(Romans 1:20)

I See You in Nature

*Magnificent, monolithic monuments
superimposed on a clear-blue sky.
Cloaked with layers of ice and snow ...
an awesome sight to the eye.
Surrounding a serene azure lake
formed by a glacial melt,
the omnipotence of You, Almighty God,
through the senses can be felt.
Nature's face is clearly reflected—
not in part, but completely.
God, You open the door to Your heart,
and You open our eyes to see.*

Anna Beth Fore

The heavens declare the glory
of God; the skies proclaim the
work of his hands. Day after day
they pour forth speech; night
after night they display knowledge.
There is no speech or language
where their voice is not heard.
(Psalm 19:1–3)

The Artist's Canvas

*In autumn You paint the trees
in many a hue
and enhance their color
with the morning dew.
Red, orange, green,
and the glitter of gold
from subtlety to brilliance
quickly unfold.
The light and the shadows
dance in the trees
as nature's ballet
performs in the breeze.
The variegated trees
reflected in lakes and streams
look impressionistic
through the sun's gleams.
The multicolored jewels fall
from the trees to the earth
where they rest and decay
then give rise to new birth.
Autumn engulfs us
and fills our senses, one and all,
as the strokes of Your genius
paint the canvas of fall.*

Anna Beth Fore

The valleys of the sea were exposed
and the foundations of the earth laid bare
at your rebuke, O Lord, at the blast of
breath from your nostrils.
(Psalm 18:15)

Nature's Path

*Winter's ice and snow melt
with spring's warming trend.
It washes a crooked path
along the earth's curves and bends.
Eons of repetition
engrave the earth's aged face,
embedding deeper wrinkles
where water leaves its trace.
Thousands of the earth's layers
revealed for our review,
providing the careful observer
with an awe-inspiring view.*

Anna Beth Fore

God's voice thunders in marvelous
ways; he does great things beyond our
understanding. He says to the snow,
"Fall on the earth," and to the rain shower,
"Be a mighty downpour." So that all men
he has made may know his work, he stops
every man from his labor. The animals
take cover; they remain in their dens.
The tempest comes out from its chamber,
the cold from the driving winds.
The breath of God produces ice, and
the broad waters become frozen.
(Job 37:5–10)

The Glacier

Mammoth blocks of ice ... thousands of years old;
deep within its bowels, many mysteries unfold.
Giant rivers of glass slowly cutting through the earth,
calving into the ocean, giving waterfalls birth.
Beautifully colored ice in rich shades of blue;
age providing the glacier with its azure hue.
Ice-covered mountaintops shaped like a cone;
massive pieces of ice breaking off on their own.
Glacial ice sculptures looking like an earthly gem;
works of such beauty could only be sculpted by Him.

As the rain and the snow come down
from heaven, and do not return to it
without watering the earth and making
it bud and flourish, so that it yields seed
for the sower and bread for the eater,
so is my word that goes out from my mouth:
It will not return to me empty, but will
accomplish what I desire and achieve
the purpose for which I sent it.
(Isaiah 55:10–11)

Snowflakes

Slowly they float to the earth,
these white flakes of manna
that quench the earth's thirst.
White and soft as the new down
of a baby gosling,
pure and unblemished
as the soul of a newborn child,
they purify the air and blanket the earth.
The trees shiver and crouch,
adorned in lovely white shawls.
The birds fly about from branch to branch
seeking warmth and refuge,
confused by yesterday's spring
and today's winter.
Slowly it comes, and slowly it melts away,
but as it vanishes from view,
it leaves the earth renewed,
bathed and refreshed to meet tomorrow.

Anna Beth Fore

Sing to the Lord with thanksgiving;
make music to our God on the harp.
He covers the sky with clouds;
he supplies the earth with rain and
makes grass grow on the hills.
(Psalm 147:7–8)

Nature's Song

The rain gently taps on my windowpane,
gray skies obscure the sun's light.
The peaceful sound of nature's refrain
playing her song as day turns to night.

The rain crescendos into a rhythmic strum;
the wind echoes its voice loud and clear.
Thunder imitates the sounds of a drum,
dancing lights in the night sky appear.

The heavens play a robust symphony.
Nature, all creatures on earth do astound.
The music of the night is a thoughtful melody,
playing heaven's most glorious sound.

Anna Beth Fore

Praise the Lord from the earth,
you great sea creatures and all ocean depths,
lightning and hail, snow and clouds,
stormy winds that do his bidding,
(Psalm 148:7–8)

The Ocean's Moods

*The earth's womb and sustainer
expresses diverse moods and emotion,
from the calm, reflective sea
to the raging, powerful ocean.*

*Sometimes the sea is joyful,
rays of sunshine dancing on her face,
seagulls gliding overhead
in a relaxed, unhurried pace.*

*Sometimes the sea is pensive,
reflective and spiritual to view.
The clouds and mist hover over her,
coloring her mood in a mystical hue.*

*Sometimes the ocean is angry,
filled with rage, power, and fight.
Her violent tidal waves and storms
display her furor and might.*

*Sometimes the ocean is playful,
gentle waves rocking boats about,
teasing man with her spontaneity
as her changing tides flow in and out.*

*The earth's womb and sustainer
expresses diverse moods and emotion,
from the calm, reflective sea,
to the raging, powerful ocean.*

Anna Beth Fore

Therefore they will be like the
morning mist, like the early dew
that disappears, like chaff swirling
from a threshing floor, like smoke
escaping through a window.
(Hosea 13:3)

Mystic Fog

The mystic fog obscures what one can see.
It plays with the mind and distorts reality.
Out of the gray, almost abysmal cloud,
the earth emerges, embraced by a dark shroud.
Silhouetted mountains against a background of gray,
illusive, opaque objects are kept at bay.
The mood is rather somber—pensive at best.
Earth's blanket around her is snugly pressed.
The real and surreal are merged into one.
Mystic fog—low clouds blocking the sun.

Anna Beth Fore

The Lord does whatever pleases him,
in the heavens and on the earth, in the seas
and all their depths. He makes clouds rise
from the ends of the earth; he sends lightning
with the rain and brings out the wind
from his storehouses.
(Psalm 135:6–7)

Rain

*The heavens are mingled with gray and black.
The air is cool and calm.
Your presence is felt as one looks toward the sky.
Nature's fireworks dance across the horizon,
and the grumblings and groans break loose
as drumrolls in thunderous applause.
The wind starts to blow as day turns to night,
and the impregnated clouds give birth to downpours,
shooting like bullets from the sky.
All nature sits in awe as the Sustainer of life
replenishes life's basic need.
And man takes shelter in a warm, cozy nook,
and watches You, our Creator, working at Your best.*

There is a time for everything,
and a season for every activity under heaven:
a time to be born and a time to die,
a time to plant and a time to uproot,
a time to kill and a time to heal,
a time to tear down and a time to build,
a time to weep and a time to laugh,
a time to mourn and a time to dance,
(Ecclesiastes 3:1–4)

Seasons of Life

The changing seasons of life rotate quickly.
Summer's long carefree days metamorphose
into autumn's cool, windy kaleidoscopes of color.
At first, the changes are slow and subtle
with only a hint of teasing blush on Nature's cheeks.
But October rains come and daylight shortens,
and soon the maple trees emerge in colorful frocks.
Nature has transformed into a mature woman.
She beckons man with her commanding presence,
and he responds with awe at her secret mysteries.
The strong rhythmic winds entice her to dance and sway
in a free, newly discovered independent way.
Soon she drops her sensual robe and bares her soul
with all its strength and earthborn scars.
Her fruit is soon gone and her bosom is bare,
and she relishes the sunlight as it fades into night.
As winter approaches, she enters a new passage.
Too soon autumn is but a memory of time passed by.

Anna Beth Fore

†

Gray hair is a crown of splendor;
it is attained by a righteous life.
(Proverbs 16:31)

Winter, the Season of Rest and Peace

The snow has fallen on your head,
the furrows of time crease your face.
Yet a smile of contentment adorns your lips
for your life reveals God's grace.

You've enjoyed the riches that life can bring,
and you've weathered the turbulent storms.
You've met the challenge of good times and bad
in both obvious and subtle forms.

Fires of temptation have tempered your soul,
and you are more precious than gold.
The sands of time have made you wise—
"a gift of age," we are told.

You've shared with us your smiles and faith,
you've given us warmth and love.
There awaits you a crown of righteousness,
a gift from our Father above.

Winter's the season of rest and peace
when you've conquered life's trials and strife.
"Gray hair is a crown of splendor;
it is attained by a righteous life."

Anna Beth Fore

Yours, O Lord, is the greatness
and the power and the glory and the majesty
and the splendor, for everything in heaven
and earth is yours. Yours, O Lord, is the kingdom;
you are exalted as head over all.
(1 Chronicles 29:11)

The Beauty of Your Creation

Father, I marvel at Your creation
as I experience its beauty and majesty.
I'm in awe of the mountains and oceans,
the flowers and trees and all that I see.

I smell the fragrance of Your plants,
and I feel wind and mist on my skin.
I'm surrounded by Your creativity,
and it stirs my creativity within.

I'm in awe of the animals You've made
and that You placed them under our reign.
I'm amazed at all of the plants You created,
how they nurture us and relieve our pain.

I gaze with wonder at Your heavens
and the vastness of the universe.
I behold the power and presence
of the planets and stars You disperse.

I'm amazed by Your ultimate creation,
man, created in the image of You.
And how You redeemed him from sin
and through Jesus made all things new.

I look forward to a new heaven and earth
when the old ones pass away.
And we have the right to the tree of life
when Your commandments we obey.

Anna Beth Fore

3

Relationships

Therefore, whoever humbles himself
like this child is the greatest in the
kingdom of heaven. And whoever
welcomes a little child like this
in my name welcomes me.
(Matthew 18:4–5)

A Precious Child

A most precious gift from You, God,
through the fertility of our seed ...
a brand new helpless miracle
filled with dependency and need.

The newborn child brings relief
as we hear the mother's sigh,
and the breath of new life begins
as we hear the baby's cry.

A look of joy and a gentle smile
adorn the mother's face
as she offers a prayer of thanksgiving
for Your amazing grace.

The father looks with amazement
as his heart beats quickly inside.
He is overwhelmed with love
as he gazes at his child with pride.

There is no greater gift
that a husband can give his wife
than the love and the union
that comes from creating life.

Created in Your image, God,
each child is totally new,
and placed on earth with purpose,
Your sovereign will to pursue.

Anna Beth Fore

Yet, O Lord, you are our Father.
We are the clay, you are the potter;
we are all the work of your hand.
(Isaiah 64:8)

The Potter and the Clay

The Potter says, "I AM the Potter, the Life, and the Way.
You are my chosen earthen vessel created from clay.
I will mold you and make you my purpose to fulfill,
and I desire your obedience and submission to my will.

If you choose to leave or forsake me, I will punish you;
but if you repent of your sins, your heart I will renew.
I'll take your broken pieces and make you whole again.
I'll purify your heart and cleanse you from all sin.

I will test you and refine you with trials through the fire.
Your obedience and submission is my greatest desire.
For I AM the Potter and you are the clay,
and my purpose for your life is to glorify The Way."

The sacrifices of God are a broken spirit;
a broken and contrite heart, O God,
you will not despise.
(Psalm 51:17)

Beautiful Stained Glass

Tiny pieces of fragmented, broken glass
stained with colors of red, yellow, and blues.
Jagged edges on different shapes and sizes,
multicolored in different shades and hues.

You, the master artisan, visualize the pile of glass,
and see a beautiful composite pattern.
You polish the glass and smooth the edges
and cause the beauty of the glass to return.

You look at the glass like a jigsaw puzzle,
each piece designed for a special place.
You carefully place the pieces side by side
until the pattern reveals a human face.

As You glue the pieces of glass together,
You nod and smile at Your work of art.
You have transformed the stained broken pieces
into a person with a pure and contrite heart.

Anna Beth Fore

The Lord is my rock, my fortress
and my deliverer; my God is my rock,
in whom I take refuge. He is my shield
and the horn of my salvation, my stronghold.
(Psalm 18:2)

My Secret Refuge

Sometimes I journey very deep down inside
to the place where my protected secrets abide.
It's a refuge for my personal self-doubts and fears,
a place where my disappointed self sheds many tears.

Around my private sanctuary are walls that protect me,
and only on rare occasions do I allow others in to see.
My child lives there, often asking "how" and "why"
do others disappoint us and loved ones often die?

When I'm hurt or wounded, I go deep inside of me.
Inside my secret refuge is the place I want to be.
It's where I can retreat and my emotions truly feel,
it's the place where I feel safe and my spirit can heal.

Anna Beth Fore

It was he who gave some to be apostles,
some to be prophets, some to be evangelists,
and some to be pastors and teachers, to prepare
God's people for works of service, so that the
body of Christ may be built up until we all reach
unity in the faith and in the knowledge of the
Son of God and become mature, attaining to the
whole measure of the fullness of Christ.
(Ephesians 4:11–13)

Pieces of the Puzzle

My life is like a jigsaw puzzle,
no two pieces are the same.
Each piece is a part of who I am
and fits somewhere in my frame.

Some of my pieces are smooth
and fit easily into place.
Some of my pieces are jagged
like the wrinkles on my face.

Sometimes the pieces are random,
and I'm not sure just where they go.
But sooner or later I can see
that they fit together "just so".

Certain pieces join together
and seem to have a theme.
Though separate, they're connected,
like a seamstress sews a seam.

Someday I'll have all the pieces,
and my puzzle will be complete.
My life will be presented to You, God,
at the feet of Your mercy seat.

Anna Beth Fore

Three times I pleaded with the Lord
to take it away from me. But he said to me,
"My grace is sufficient for you, for my power
is made perfect in weakness." Therefore I
will boast all the more gladly about my weaknesses,
so that Christ's power may rest on me.
That is why, for Christ's sake, I delight in
weaknesses, in insults, in hardships,
in persecutions, in difficulties. For when
I am weak, then I am strong.
(2 Corinthians 12:8–10)

In My Weakness

As I lay still, flat on my back
on a cold, compactly tiled floor,
my semi-conscious body was motionless
under the bedroom and bathroom door.
I felt pain in my neck, back, and arms,
and my body was helpless and weak.
There was a throbbing in my forehead,
and blood trickled from a cut on my cheek.
I heard the voice of my husband,
and the paramedics were talking to me,
but the sounds seemed distant and far away
as they tried to determine my coherency.
They placed a brace around my neck
and moved me onto a hard, straight board.
Then they transported me in the dreary rain
to an ambulance and secured me on board.
The ride was bumpy and shaky,
and I was turned to vomit on the floor.
My body was cold and trembling
as we passed through the emergency room door.
Then came the questions and tests
as they examined every part of me,
but a drink of water and a softer bed
was my body's heartfelt plea.
I was totally dependent on others
as they ministered and cared for me,
and my mind and heart cried out to You, God,
to give me strength in my agony.
It was in these moments of helplessness
as I looked into a concerned, caring face,
that I understood that man's total dependency
magnifies Your unsurpassable grace.
In my weakness, You are made strong!
Thank You, Lord!

Anna Beth Fore

"For I know the plans I have for you,"
declares the Lord, "plans to prosper you
and not to harm you, plans to give you
hope and a future".
(Jeremiah 29:11)

Your Destiny for Me, Lord

Where was I when You created the foundation of the earth?
Where was I when You formed Adam from a lump of clay?
Where was I when You knew me in the womb before my birth?
Who am I to question Your authority—rather than to obey?

No human being can understand what goes on under the sun.
Despite his knowledge and efforts, no man can comprehend.
There are endless mysteries to challenge the minds of everyone.
Every endeavor is meaningless—a chasing after the wind!

No one knows the future, but we all share a common destiny,
Both the righteous and the wicked, the clean and the unclean.
Everyone experiences joy, suffering, heartache, and enmity.
And though prophecies forewarn—their meaning is not seen.

God, You alone are in control—You rule over the universe.
Your desire for me is to fear You, revere You, to trust You and obey,
To worship You, to glorify You, and in prayer with You converse,
and in humble submission, live my life to conform to Your way!

Anna Beth Fore

I have set my rainbow in the clouds,
and it will be the sign of the covenant
between me and the earth. Whenever I
bring clouds over the earth and the rainbow
appears in the clouds, I will remember
my covenant between me and you
and all living creatures of every kind.
Never again will the waters
become a flood to destroy all life.
(Genesis 9:13–15)

The Rainbow

After the storm, a calm reappears.
The clouds emptied, the sky clears.
The air smells fresh, pure, and clean.
Birds that have hidden can now be seen.
Puddles of rain everywhere abound.
Droplets from treetops still fall to the ground.
A multicolored arc paints the horizon.
From out of the clouds peeks the sun.
A sign from You, God, that never again
will You destroy the world by water because of sin.

Anna Beth Fore

For this reason Christ is the mediator of a new covenant, that those who are called may receive the promised eternal inheritance—now that he has died as a ransom to set them free from the sins committed under the first covenant.
(Hebrews 9:15)

An Heir of Your Covenants, God

I am an heir of Your covenant with Noah ...
a majestic rainbow set in the clouds,
that never again will a flood destroy all life,
nor its waters the earth wholly enshroud.

I am an heir of Your covenant with Abraham ...
who became the father of many nations.
You made an everlasting covenant to be his God
and the God of all future generations.

I am an heir of Your covenant with Isaac ...
who would be blessed through Sarah, his mother.
You established Your everlasting covenant with Isaac,
blessing him more than Ishmael, his brother.

I am an heir of Your covenant with Jacob ...
to receive the land of Canaan as his portion.
Through his descendants, his twelve sons,
You kept Your covenant to the chosen ones.

I am an heir of Your covenant with Moses ...
to whom You spoke at a mountain place.
You gave him the Ten Commandments on stone,
and he descended Mount Sinai with a radiant face.

I am an heir of Your new covenant
through the blood of Jesus Christ, Your son.
This covenant promises eternal life
to all of Your heirs when the victory is won!

Anna Beth Fore

4

Jesus

Suddenly a great company of the heavenly
host appeared with the angel, praising God and saying,
"Glory to God in the highest, and on earth
peace to men on whom his favor rests."
(Luke 2:13–14)

The Angels' Proclamation

Hallelujah! Hallelujah!
Let us praise His holy name!
For "He is the Savior",
all the angels proclaim.
Let all the heavenly hosts rejoice
in heaven and on earth.
For on this blessed day,
we witness our Savior's birth.
He is the Messiah
who was prophesied before.
He is the King of Kings
whom we praise and adore.
Let us play the trumpets loudly
so that all will hear the call.
The Prince of Peace and Lord of Lords
has come to save us all.

Anna Beth Fore

And Mary said: "My soul glorifies the Lord and my spirit rejoices in God my Savior, for he has been mindful of the humble state of his servant. From now on all generations will call me blessed, for the Mighty One has done great things for me—holy is his name".
(Luke 1:46–49)

Mary

A young teenage virgin
chosen by You, God Almighty,
to give birth to a Savior
who would set all men free.
Mary glorified You, Lord,
with a servant's humility
and knew You had blessed her
for all generations to see.
She gave birth to Jesus
and raised her Jewish boy.
She knew that her son
would bring the world joy.
As Jesus grew into a man,
Mary was always near.
She knew He was the Messiah
whom everyone should fear.
She was present at the wedding
when He turned water into wine.
She likely heard Him teach,
"You are the branches, I am the vine."
Mary was present at the cross
when Jesus was crucified,
and she and John and others
were with Him when He died.
She saw His resurrected body
after He rose from the grave.
She knew that Your dear son
was the only one who could save.
Mary has been called blessed
from generation to generation,
for You, God, did great things for her
as the mother of Jesus, her son.

Anna Beth Fore

For to us a child is born, to us a son
is given, and the government will be on
his shoulders. And he will be called
Wonderful Counselor, Mighty God,
Everlasting Father, Prince of Peace.
(Isaiah 9:6)

A Blessing for Peace

*It came to pass on that first Christmas morn,
that You, God, sent Your only Son from heaven.
"For unto us a child is born;
unto us a son is given."
His name shall be called Wonderful Counselor,
The Mighty God, and the Prince of Peace.
Jesus Christ, whom we worship and adore,
gives us life, and from death gives us release.
He gives us His peace at all times,
in every way,
if we believe Him and abide in His will.
He gives us joy, hope, and peace every day
when we take time to be quiet and still.
May the Prince of Peace
bless each one of our families
as we enjoy His gift from above.
And may we live in peace and harmony
so that all men will see His love.*

Anna Beth Fore

Praise be to the God and Father of our
Lord Jesus Christ, who has blessed us
in the heavenly realms with every spiritual
blessing in Christ. For he chose us in him
before the creation of the world to be holy
and blameless in his sight. In love he
predestined us to be adopted as his sons
through Jesus Christ, in accordance
with his pleasure and will—
to the praise of his glorious grace,
which he has freely given us
in the One he loves.
(Ephesians 1:3–6)

God's Precious Gift

*The wayward child
hides his shameful face
and turns away
from the Savior's grace.
But You, Almighty God,
pursue the sinful one
and offer him the gift
of a Savior, Your precious son.
The humbled child
sheds remorseful tears
and his father's arms
relieve his fears.
He shouts with joy
at his sins' release
and You fill his heart
with an inner peace.
God, Your gift is free
to all of us who believe,
who open our hearts
and gladly receive.
The gift of Jesus
who took our place
brings us joy and hope
through Your amazing grace!*

And the peace of God, which transcends
all understanding, will guard your hearts
and your minds in Christ Jesus.
(Philippians 4:7)

The Prince of Peace

*Jesus, the Prince of Peace, breathes grace
on all of us who will gladly receive.
He promises us joy and peace
beyond understanding
if we have faith in Him and believe.
He is the shepherd who leads us
beside still waters,
who meets our needs and restores our soul.
He is the bread of life and the water
that quenches our thirst,
who fills us with His spirit,
and makes our hearts whole.
May we be still and quiet
and know that He is God,
as we behold His holy and radiant face.
And may we feel the breath
of the Prince of Peace
as He breathes on us
His mercy and grace.*

Anna Beth Fore

One day Jesus said to his disciples, "Let's go over to the other side of the lake." So they got into a boat and set out. As they sailed, he fell asleep. A squall came down on the lake, so that the boat was being swamped, and they were in great danger. The disciples went and woke him, saying, "Master, Master, we're going to drown!" He got up and rebuked the wind and the raging waters; the storm subsided, and all was calm.
(Luke 8:22–24)

Master of the Sea

Sometimes I feel like a solitary sailboat
adrift in a vast, mighty ocean,
wandering to and fro with the wind,
through mist and fog and veiled sun.

It seems there is little direction,
and I don't know what my course should be.
The darkness of night dims my perspective,
and makes it difficult for me to see.

But then I remember what You said, Master,
that You will never leave or forsake me,
and I feel peace and comfort in Your presence
as You take the helm on the mighty sea.

You change my course in a new direction
and lead me toward a safe harbor.
When You control the sails in the winds,
I feel protected, safe, and secure.

The winds and the weather remain the same
but my master has set me free.
It is no longer I who control the helm
but my master who lives in me.

He heals the brokenhearted
and binds up their wounds.
(Psalm 147:3)

Jesus Heals our Broken Hearts

In the heart of every man,
buried deeply within,
lies the shame and disgust
that comes from secret sin.
Our sin is hidden and protected
in this private retreat,
but it festers and poisons us
with its toxic deceit.
These dark, ugly secrets
cause man's heart to be torn,
but they prompt the heart of Jesus
to weep, wail, and mourn.
He desires that man will confess his sins
and then humbly repent,
because this is why Jesus, our Savior,
to the earth was sent.
Man, in his imperfect state, is sinful
along with all of humanity,
so You, God, sent Your perfect son
to rescue us with His divinity.
God, You desire that we believe in Him
and submit to His almighty will,
then He will forgive us our sins,
and our broken hearts He will heal.

Anna Beth Fore

Let us fix our eyes on Jesus,
the author and perfecter of our
faith, who for the joy set before
him endured the cross, scorning
its shame, and sat down at the right
hand of the throne of God.
(Hebrews 12:2)

A Personal Look at the Cross

As I look at the cross with my head bowed low,
feelings of both joy and sorrow in my heart overflow.
I think of You, Almighty God, who sent Your son to this earth
to experience humanity through His immaculate birth.
The God of the universe who loves me so much
sent His son so that I could be healed by His touch.
A perfect and holy Savior lived a life of purity
and sacrificed His life to forgive and sanctify me.
How lonely and vulnerable He must have felt on the cross,
bearing the sins of the world as His human life He lost.
My heart is broken and cries out in humility,
but my spirit rejoices because He set my soul free!
He opens my eyes and gives me new eyes to see
that my purpose here is to serve others in peace and unity.
He opens my ears to hear His voice and His call,
to praise and honor Him by sharing His message with all.
He opens my mouth to praise Him in word and in song,
and to speak kind, loving words to others all day long.
He opens my heart to the poor, the lonely,
and the depressed,
and He asks me to serve them and to give them my best.
As I look at the cross, I see beyond it an empty grave,
as Christ triumphed over death and my life He did save!
There's victory in Jesus' resurrection,
and the battle is won
as You conquered sin and evil through the blood of Your son.
And now I have the gift of salvation
and the hope of eternity,
and I know that Your Holy Spirit is living in me.
Thank You, God, that the cross reminds me every day
that You are my Savior, the truth, and The Way.

Anna Beth Fore

It is for freedom that Christ has set
us free. Stand firm, then, and do not
let yourselves be burdened again by
a yoke of slavery.
(Galatians 5:1)

Thank You for Freeing Me

*I was enslaved to selfishness and pride
as I struggled with sin and strife,
but You freed me, Jesus, when You died,
and Your resurrection gave me new life.*

*I once was bound to fleshly desires,
seeking things that would satisfy me,
but You tempered me through many fires
and created me for a unique destiny.*

*I was enticed by earthly pleasures
and blinded by Satan's wily deceit,
but You taught me about heaven's treasures
when You washed Your disciples' feet.*

*I was humbled when You loved me
and died to release me from sin.
Jesus, thank You for setting me free
and filling me with God's Spirit within.*

*Jesus, thank You for removing the chains
through Your most amazing grace.
I long to be in heaven under Your reign
where I will see Your radiant face.*

Anna Beth Fore

So do not be ashamed to testify about our Lord, or ashamed of me his prisoner. But join with me in suffering for the gospel, by the power of God, who has saved us and called us to a holy life—not because of anything we have done but because of his own purpose and grace. This grace was given us in Christ Jesus before the beginning of time, but it has now been revealed through the appearing of our Savior, Christ Jesus, who has destroyed death and has brought life and immortality to light through the gospel.
(2 Timothy 1:8–10)

The Greatest Gift

The greatest gift we will ever receive is love,
wrapped in forgiveness and grace
from You, our Father above.
Jesus Christ was given to us
by You, the highest and utmost,
and praise and honor accompanied Him
by the heavenly host.
Christ was born in Bethlehem,
and in a lowly manger He lay;
but the King of Kings and Lord of Lords
was born on that special day.
Unto us a Savior was born
in the gift of a human baby boy,
and He would bring the world
peace, love, hope, and joy.
Love is also the greatest gift
we can give to one another,
wrapped in joy and mercy
and shared with each other.

When they came to the place called the Skull, there they crucified him, along with the criminals—one on his right, the other on his left. Jesus said, "Father, forgive them, for they do not know what they are doing".
(Luke 23:33–34)

The Cross

*It was on the cross at Calvary where Jesus cried,
"Father, forgive them, they know not what they do".
It was for the sins of all mankind that He died
and triumphed over death and made all things new.
The blood He shed was the atonement for all sin
as He willingly sacrificed Himself to a cruel death.
He paid the price of redemption for all men
as He cried out to You, God, and took His last breath.
He was buried in a tomb and arose the third day
and appeared to His disciples so that they could see.
He showed them He was the true and living way
and promised believers a life in heaven for eternity.*

†

Now we see but a poor reflection
as in a mirror; then we shall see
face to face. Now I know in part;
then I shall know fully,
even as I am fully known.
(1 Corinthians 13:12)

The Reflection of Jesus

What do I see when I look in a mirrored glass?
The reflection of Your glory, God, that nothing can surpass!
The veil from the old covenant has been taken away;
when we turn to You, Lord, You show us the way.
I see no blemish, no sin, no blight or imperfection—
I see a glorious transformation because of Jesus, Your Son.
Once I was enslaved to pride, sinful pleasure, and greedy gain,
but this selfish indulgence resulted in misery and pain.
I believe in You, God, and I know Your Spirit has set me free.
Now I live to reflect Your glory, Lord, for everyone to see.
As I look intently into Your perfect law of freedom and grace,
I see the reflection of Jesus in my heart and on my face!

Anna Beth Fore

Now to him who is able to do immeasurably more than all we ask or imagine, according to his power that is at work within us, to him be glory in the church and in Christ Jesus throughout all generations, forever and ever! Amen.
(Ephesians 3:20–21)

Jesus Is the Extra in My Extraordinary Life

*God, You created me uniquely
as a beautiful work of art.
You sculpted my body from clay
to protect my sacred heart.
When I submit my will to You,
You set my spirit free,
and Your love and grace is all-sufficient
when I bow on bended knee.
The time I spend with Jesus
draws Him even closer to me,
and when I place my trust in Him,
we share unsurpassable intimacy.
When I choose to obey Jesus
because of His sacrifice and grace,
He fills my life with blessings and promises
that I will someday see His face.
God, You long for me to know You,
but I must wait patiently and be still.
And through Your Word and Holy Spirit,
You will reveal Your sovereign will.
God, You will not bestow upon me
my every earthly desire,
but You will make me extraordinary
as You refine me with Your fire.
It is no longer I who live,
but it is Christ who lives in me.
And He is the extra in my ordinary life
that I want the world to see!*

Anna Beth Fore

5

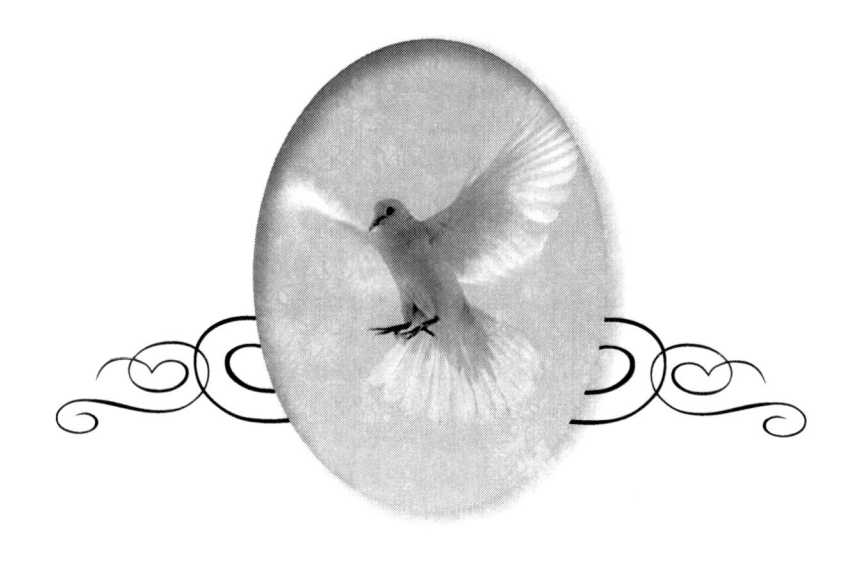

God's Holy Spirit

†

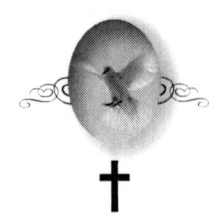

I pray that out of his glorious riches
he may strengthen you with power
through his Spirit in your inner being,
so that Christ may dwell in your hearts
through faith. And I pray that you,
being rooted and established in love,
may have power, together with all the
saints, to grasp how wide and long and
high and deep is the love of Christ,
and to know this love that surpasses
knowledge—that you may be filled
to the measure of all the
fullness of God.
(Ephesians 3:16–19)

The Spirit of God

*Deep within the Christian
where the soul lives inside,
Your vibrant Holy Spirit, God,
does also abide.
The Spirit is there to comfort us
when life falls apart.
The Spirit is there to mend us
when we have a broken heart.
The Spirit encourages us
when we're filled with self-doubt—
and when we pause to ponder
what life is all about.
The Spirit gives us peace
amid hostility and war.
The Spirit gives us joy
and a purpose to live for.
The Spirit guides our lives
in the decisions that we make—
and directs our feet
in the paths that we take.
Your Spirit, God, within us
sets our souls and spirits free,
and inspires believers
to become all that we can be.*

Anna Beth Fore

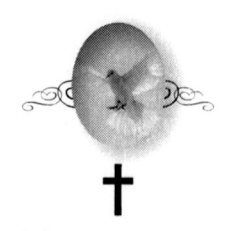

For you did not receive a spirit that
makes you a slave again to fear, but
you received the Spirit of sonship.
And by him we cry, "Abba, Father."
(Romans 8:15)

Abba, Father
(a plea for intimacy)

Abba, Father, how I long to know You,
to truly seek You with all of my heart and being.
I want to gaze upon Your glory and majesty
with eyes full of awe and praise and perceiving.

Envelop me with the sunlight of Your presence,
and let me feel Your warmth on every part of my skin.
Fill my emptiness with the fire of Your Holy Spirit,
and make me feel warm and glow from within.

Let me soak up Your goodness and love
like a sponge that absorbs water, pure and clean.
Open my eyes to Your spiritual mysteries,
and reveal Your truths about the world unseen.

Make me a harmonious chord in nature's symphony,
and keep me in tune with Your awesome creation.
Help me follow Your leadership as I sing praise to You
and shout "Hallelujah" to You and to Jesus, Your son.

Search, cleanse, and refine my heart, Abba Father,
so that I am pure and holy in Your sight.
Guide me, encourage me, and empower me, Father—
let Your Holy Spirit strengthen me with His might.

Abba, Father, I long to know and be known by You,
to truly come into Your presence and be still.
As I yearn for You and seek intimacy with You,
give me grace and faith to submit to Your will.

Anna Beth Fore

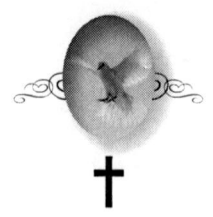

"Whoever believes in me, as the
scripture has said, streams of living water
will flow from within him."
By this he meant the Spirit, whom those
who believed in him were later to receive.
Up to that time the Spirit had not been
given, since Jesus had not yet
been glorified.
(John 7:38–39)

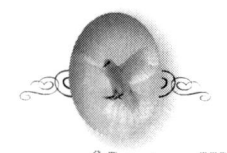

Streams of Living Water

Just as cold, clean, pure, flowing water
sustains man's human vitality,
so the Holy Spirit's streams of living water
renew our inner man's spirituality.
Man has a nagging thirst and inner longing
to know You, the God of all creation,
who can quench our thirst and satisfy our needs
through Your indwelling Spirit
and the gift of Jesus, Your Son.
These refreshing streams of living water
rise up in our spirits like water from a spring,
and they strengthen us and nourish us
and revive us in the songs that we sing.
The living water cleanses us and purifies us
and gives us the Holy Spirit's power within.
It gives us the desire and strength to imitate Christ
and the power and might to defeat Satan and sin.
The fruit produced from these streams of living water
will glorify You, God, as others witness them in me,
and I will enjoy peace, joy, love, and hope
as Your Holy Spirit dwells with me for eternity.

Anna Beth Fore

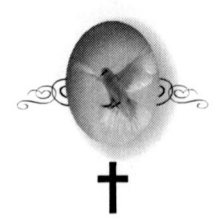

And we, who with unveiled faces
all reflect the Lord's glory,
are being transformed into his likeness
with ever-increasing glory,
which comes from the Lord, who is the Spirit.
(2 Corinthians 3:18)

Transformation

As a caterpillar emerges from its safe cocoon,
so a human being breaks free from its mother's womb.
As a caterpillar is transformed into a beautiful butterfly,
so the spirit of man is transformed by the empty tomb.
Jesus takes the common, the ordinary, the average face,
and He makes it uncommon and extraordinary
by His redeeming grace.
God, Your Holy Spirit provides sweet nectar and nourishment
from nature's sweet, fragrant flowers
and offers it freely to everyone who believes—
and His presence within is the gift that empowers.
At first, the caterpillar crawls awkwardly and slowly,
limited in its mobility from place to place.
But the transformed butterfly flies gracefully and freely,
seemingly uninhibited by time and space.
In the same way, man's spirit is miraculously transformed
from humanity's attraction to self and sin,
to a new life of service and self-sacrifice to our King
who transforms us by His Holy Spirit from deep within.

Anna Beth Fore

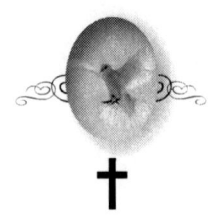

The Spirit of God has made me;
the breath of the Almighty gives me life.
(Job 33:4)

The Breath of Life

*Almighty God, You breathe the breath of life
into those who obey You and repent of their sin.
You breathe life through Your Holy Spirit
who gives light and truth to Christians within.*

*The unsurpassed power of Your Holy Spirit
imparts the truth to man through His breath
and enables him to be a witness for You, God,
releasing him from the power of sin and death.*

*The Holy Spirit provides comfort and peace
to those who believe in Jesus Christ, Your son,
and He produces the fruit of love and patience,
peace and godliness, in the lives of every Christian.*

*God, You breathe hope and joy into the spirit of man
and transform him so that all may see
that the believer is an heir of salvation
and will live with You in heaven for eternity.*

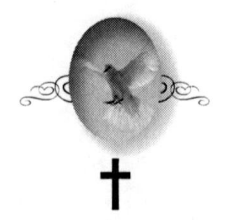

But the fruit of the Spirit is love, joy, peace, patience, kindness, goodness, faithfulness, gentleness and self-control. Against such things there is no law. Those who belong to Christ Jesus have crucified the sinful nature with its passions and desires. Since we live by the Spirit, let us keep in step with the Spirit.
(Galatians 5:22–25)

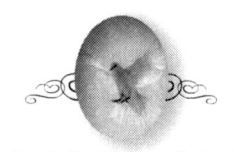

Make Me Fruitful, Lord

Your Holy Spirit lives in me, Lord.
He is my strength and Counselor.
He reveals Your truth and sets me free
and gives me eagles' wings to soar.

Give me a good attitude, Lord,
a heart filled with love, joy, and peace.
Help me to overlook others' offenses
and through forgiveness give them release.

Help me to live out Your fruits, Lord,
through patience, kindness, and goodness,
and to submit to Your will in every thing,
and be assured that my life You will bless.

Help me to empty myself of my desires
and free me from the attraction of sin.
Fill me up with Your goodness, Lord,
and empower me from within.

Make me faithful and gentle, Lord,
and strengthen me with self-control.
Surround me with Your holiness, Lord;
give me a thankful and humble soul.

Make me strong in my weaknesses, Lord,
in all that I say and do.
May Your Holy Spirit make me fruitful
and transform me into the likeness of You.

Anna Beth Fore

6

Shouts in the Storm

Those who sow in tears
will reap with songs of joy.
He who goes out weeping,
carrying seed to sow, will
return with songs of joy,
carrying sheaves with him.
(Psalm 126:5–6)

Tears of Sorrow

*I weep easily this morning
and I don't know why,
but the tears flow freely
as I sob and cry.
I look all around me
and see others with more pain.
Nonetheless, I can't stop weeping
nor my emotions restrain.*

*I feel a common bond
with all who suffer and endure
from diseases and illnesses
for which there is no cure.
I feel a sense of helplessness
for those who suffer and despair,
for those who are brokenhearted
and have many burdens to bear.*

*As we worship together
as a family in community,
we are bound by Jesus' love
in our faith and unity.
As we sing and pray together
in harmony with each other,
God, Your spirit gives us strength
to honor You and one another.*

*As I weep these tears of sorrow
You carry the pain for me,
and I feel Your peace and comfort
as You cover me lovingly.*

Anna Beth Fore

When my heart was grieved
and my spirit embittered, I was
senseless and ignorant; I was
a brute beast before you. Yet
I am always with you; you hold
me by my right hand. You guide
me with your counsel, and afterward
you will take me into glory.
(Psalm 73:21-24)

A Broken Heart

I'm completely broken, Lord,
and my world is falling apart.
I can't control or fix things,
and I have a broken heart.

I feel helpless and hopeless,
and I don't see You anywhere.
I cry out to You in desperation,
and I hope that You are there.

I want to feel Your presence, Lord,
though my eyes are filled with tears.
I want to remember the blessings
You've given throughout the years.

Help me be steadfast and patient
and to endure this suffering.
Help me to ask for the strength
that only Your Spirit can bring.

Hold me close this morning, Lord,
and help me through this day.
Renew my strength and hope,
and lead me on my way.

Mend my heart, dear Lord,
and fill it with humility.
Put words of praise on my lips
for Your faithfulness to me.

Anna Beth Fore

Therefore do not let sin reign in your
mortal body so that you obey its evil desires.
Do not offer the parts of your body to sin,
as instruments of wickedness, but rather
offer yourselves to God, as those who have
been brought from death to life; and offer
the parts of your body to him as
instruments of righteousness.
(Romans 6:12–13)

Entangled in Sin

Beautiful and alluring, enticing and inviting
is the outward adornment of sin.
The call of Your spirit and the cry of our natural man
cause fierce battles and struggles within.
Satan weaves delicate, imperceptible threads
into a finely woven web of deceit.
He places his web in front of a delicious treat,
then entangles his victims in a trap of defeat.
At first we struggle back and forth
trying to free ourselves from his hold,
but the more we resist, the more he pursues,
becoming more brazen and bold.
We find ourselves deeply entangled,
staring our enemy square in the face.
It is then that we cry out in desperation,
confessing our sins and seeking Your grace.
Almighty God, our Lord and Savior,
You hear our call and answer our plea.
You cut the threads and cords that bind us
and forgive our sins and set us free.
When we call on You, Lord and Savior,
when Satan entices us with sin,
we have the assurance from You, Almighty God,
that You alone have the power to win!

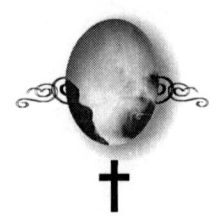

Then he said to me, "Prophesy
to these bones and say to them,
'Dry bones, hear the word of the Lord!
This is what the Sovereign Lord says
to these bones: I will make breath
enter you, and you will come to life.
I will attach tendons to you and make
flesh come upon you and cover you
with skin; I will put breath in you,
and you will come to life. Then you
will know that I am the Lord.'"
(Ezekiel 37:4–6)

Dry Bones in the Desert

Sometimes I feel parched in the desert
surrounded by piles of dry bones.
Sometimes I am starving and thirsty,
but there is nothing to eat but hard stones.

Sometimes there is no life within me,
the breath of life has been taken away.
I have no source of food to sustain me,
no strength or energy for the day.

I lie lifeless in a pile of dry bones
with no purpose or meaning to life.
I feel nothing . . . no love, joy, or hope,
not even feelings of anger or strife.

But God pursues me in the desert
and resurrects me from my death.
He restores the flesh on my bones,
giving new life with His Spirit's breath.

God restores our broken relationship
and leads me out of the night.
He gives me water and food and air
and warms me with His light.

God reignites His fire within me
and causes my face and spirit to glow.
He is the source of my life and passion
from whom all my blessings flow.

Anna Beth Fore

I have come into the world as a light,
so that no one who believes in me
should stay in darkness.
(John 12:46)

In the Darkness

In the gloomy darkness,
I experience much pain.
There is no sunshine,
only steady torrential rain.

As I try to walk around,
I stumble for I cannot see.
I feel around for objects
to support and steady me.

I imagine fearful things
contrived by the Enemy.
My thoughts are in bondage,
and despair is my reality.

I cry out to You, Almighty God,
with tearful moans and sighs.
I plead with You to free me
from Satan's powerful lies.

I speak the name of Jesus
who is always there for me.
He is my Savior and Redeemer.
He alone can set me free.

In the gloomy darkness
that engulfs me in the night.
I declare the name of Jesus
who leads me by His light.

This is what the Lord says:
"Heaven is my throne, and the earth
is my footstool. Where is the house
you will build for me? Where will
my resting place be? Has not my
hand made all these things, and so they
came into being?" declares the Lord.
"This is the one I esteem: he who is
humble and contrite in spirit, and
trembles at my word."
(Isaiah 66:1-2)

On Bended Knee

So many times I seek to be self-sufficient,
and my heart is filled with pride.
Outwardly, I feign humility and submission,
but my controlling nature I cannot hide.

When my idol is independence and strength,
I cannot clearly see Your face.
I credit myself with life's successes,
instead of You, God, for Your amazing grace.

Too often my pride and sinful self
are unwilling to confess my sins and forgive.
Too often I'm unwilling to submit to another
and encourage them to thrive and live.

Foolish pride goes before destruction
and a haughty spirit before a fall.
But wisdom cries out for humility
when I listen to the Spirit's call.

Let me seek Your heart and will, God,
when I pray fervently on bended knee.
May You transform me into Your likeness
to reflect Your glory living in me.

Anna Beth Fore

I call on you, O God, for you will answer me; give ear to me and hear my prayer. Show the wonder of your great love, you who save by your right hand those who take refuge in you from their foes.
(Psalm 17:6–7)

Hear Our Prayer, Lord

Dear Lord, our hearts are broken,
and the pain seems too much to bear.
Let Your Holy Spirit cry out for us
as we come to You in prayer.
This precious child, a gift from You,
has been tragically taken away.
We mourn and weep and grieve for him
each moment of each day.
The loss of this precious child, Lord,
cuts through to our very soul.
Please wrap Your arms around us
as You comfort and console.
Thank you, Lord, for this child,
Your gift of joy and delight.
We know how much You love him,
that he is precious in Your sight.
We know that this child is safe in Your arms
because we know that Your words are true,
and that he is smiling and playing
in his new heavenly home with You.
Thank you for sharing this precious one
with us for a little while.
Help us remember the love and joy
he gave us with his smile.
We pray for peace and comfort, Lord,
as we face each difficult day.
We ask for compassion and strength
as we come to You and pray.

Anna Beth Fore

I say to myself, "The Lord is my portion;
therefore I will wait for him." The Lord is good
to those whose hope is in him, to the one who
seeks him; it is good to wait quietly for
the salvation of the Lord.
(Lamentations 3:24–26)

In the Stillness

It's very still and quiet here
alone in the middle of the night.
I'm anxious with doubts and fears,
and there's no one else in sight.

The pain in my body cries out,
and I seem to find no relief.
My mind is filled with doubt
as I question my belief.

Why must my body suffer so?
Do You really hear my prayer?
How can I really know?
Are You really there?

I do believe You love me,
and I want to trust in You.
I want to have faith
that Your promises are true.

I want Your strength
and Your peace living in me.
I want my sufferings
to increase my humility.

I want to call on Your name
and know that You really care.
I want the Spirit to groan for me
and to know that You are there.

Please help me hear Your voice,
and open my eyes to see.
Please comfort me in the stillness,
and take these fears from me.

Anna Beth Fore

And I pray that you, being rooted
and established in love, may have
power, together with all the saints,
to grasp how wide and long and high
and deep is the love of Christ, and to
know this love that surpasses knowledge—
that you may be filled to the measure
of all the fullness of God.
Ephesians 3:17-19

The Fears of Aging

My world is changing, Lord,
as my friends and loved ones die.
It seems that I am left here alone
as I whisper another "good-bye".

My world is shrinking, Lord,
and I cannot go out as much.
I struggle through another day
without any human touch.

My world is frightening, Lord,
and I am forgetful and confused.
I can't remember names and dates,
and important things I often lose.

My world is very lonely, Lord,
as I live in my house alone.
Some days I don't see anyone,
and my nearest friend is my phone.

But You, O Lord, are my Father,
and You are my dearest friend.
Even though my world is changing
on You I can always depend.

You will sit beside me, Lord,
throughout my darkest night.
You will hold my hand, Lord,
and warm me with Your light.

You will give me peace, Lord,
and remove all of my fears.
Put Your arms around me, Lord,
and wipe away my tears.

Anna Beth Fore

"The pillars of the heavens quake,
aghast at his rebuke. By his power
he churned up the sea; by his wisdom
he cut Rahab to pieces. By his breath
the skies became fair; his hand pierced
the gliding serpent. And these are but
the outer fringe of his works; how faint
the whisper we hear of him! Who then
can understand the thunder of his power?"
(Job 26:11–14)

I Hear Your Voice, Lord

I hear Your loud voice, Lord,
when hurricanes topple the trees.
I hear Your soft voice, Lord,
when the wind hums in the breeze.

I hear Your bold voice, Lord,
when You declare Your authority.
I hear Your gentle voice, Lord,
when You encourage me lovingly.

I hear Your powerful voice, Lord,
when You tell me to submit to Your will.
I hear Your patient voice, Lord,
when You tell me to wait and be still.

I hear Your reprimanding voice, Lord,
when You tell me to revere You and obey.
I hear Your compassionate voice, Lord,
when You hear the words that I pray.

I hear Your authoritative voice, Lord,
when You declare Your sovereignty.
I hear Your reassuring voice, Lord,
when You say You will never leave me.

I hear Your triumphant voice, Lord,
when You proclaim Your victory.
I hear Your joyful voice, Lord,
when You take me home for eternity.

Anna Beth Fore

You are my hiding place; you will
protect me from trouble and surround me
with songs of deliverance. Selah.
(Psalm 32:7)

Surround Me, Lord

Surround me, Lord, with Your presence
each minute and hour of each day.
Shine Your light in this world's darkness,
and guide my feet on Your pathway.

There are evil forces compelling me
to deny Your power and might,
and Satan uses his deceitful lies
to mask and diffuse Your light.

My flesh desires human pleasures,
and Satan tempts me with pride.
He tries to persuade me to please myself
and to hide my secret sins inside.

There are spiritual powers at war, Lord,
causing anger, revenge, and strife.
There are demons disguised as angels
who are struggling to control my life.

Help me call on the name of Jesus, Lord,
when Your enemies seek to entrap me.
Help me submit to You and resist them,
and through faith and grace set me free.

Surround me, Lord, with Your presence
each minute and hour of each day.
Shine Your light in this world's darkness,
and guide my feet on Your pathway.

Anna Beth Fore

Do not conform any longer
to the pattern of this world, but be transformed
by the renewing of your mind.
Then you will be able to test and approve
what God's will is—
his good, pleasing and perfect will.
(Romans 12:2)

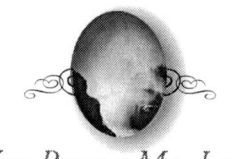

You Renew Me, Lord

Sometimes I'm filled with anxiety and fear,
and I try to control the situation,
instead of humbling myself on my knees
and asking for the grace of Your Son.

Sometimes I'm overwhelmed with life
with its difficulties and daily demands,
and then the Holy Spirit reminds me
that my life is safe in Your hands.

Sometimes I think that I'm all alone,
that every one has forgotten about me,
and then I recall that You are my friend
who gives me peace and serenity.

Sometimes I feel that my life is empty
and there's a huge void in my soul,
and then I hear Your loving voice
whispering, "I will make you whole".

Sometimes I am weary and tired,
and I feel depressed and blue,
but when I'm still and I wait on You,
my strength You will renew.

Sometimes I'm filled with gratitude,
and I sing praise to the one I adore.
Then I soar on wings like eagles
for I'll be in Your presence evermore.

Anna Beth Fore

Submit yourselves, then, to God.
Resist the devil, and he will flee from you.
Come near to God and he will come
near to you. Wash your hands,
you sinners, and purify your hearts,
you double-minded. Grieve, mourn and
wail. Change your laughter to mourning
and your joy to gloom. Humble yourselves
before the Lord, and he will lift you up.
(James 4:7-10)

Help Me Surrender, Lord

Lord, help me surrender to You
in every thing I say and do.
Help me empty myself of me,
and make my life one of humility.

Help me give up all of my pride
and ask Your Spirit to be my guide.
Help me willingly give up my sin,
resist Satan, and remain holy within.

Remind me always of Your sacrifice—
my salvation was bought with a price.
Remind me of Your love for me—
Your death on the cross set me free.

Remind me that You came to serve,
to give me a life I don't deserve.
Remind me of how You want me to live—
to love others, to be kind, and to forgive.

Help me surrender myself completely
so that every person will see
that I have died to my sinful self,
and Jesus Christ is living in me.

Anna Beth Fore

The teachers of the law and the
Pharisees brought in a woman caught
in adultery. They made her stand
before the group and said to Jesus,
"Teacher, this woman was caught in the act
of adultery. In the Law Moses commanded us
to stone such women. Now what do you say?"
They were using this question as a trap,
in order to have a basis for accusing him.
But Jesus bent down and started to write
on the ground with his finger.
When they kept on questioning him,
he straightened up and said to them,
"If any one of you is without sin,
let him be the first to throw
a stone at her."
(John 8:3–7)

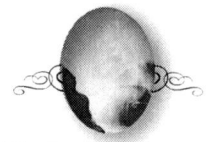

We Are All the Adulterous Woman

We are all the adulterous woman, Lord,
sharing lives that are filled with sin.
Our lives are exposed and made vulnerable
in Your presence and the presence of men.

We are all the adulterous woman, Lord,
stripped in shame without dignity,
for we all give in to our fleshly desires
and are brought to our knees in humility.

We are all the adulterous woman, Lord,
and we bow our heads in disgrace,
for we fear the look of disgust and scorn
that we think we will see on Your face.

We are all the adulterous woman, Lord,
as we witness You writing in the sand.
We look up and see that everyone is gone
as You reach out to us with Your hand.

We are all the adulterous woman, Lord,
as we see the love and hope in Your eyes.
We receive Your grace and forgiveness,
and repent as our flesh we deny.

We are all the adulterous woman, Lord,
whom You tell to go and sin no more.
We rise up from the dirt and go on our way
singing praises to You, the one we adore.

Anna Beth Fore

"Come to me, all you who are weary and burdened,
and I will give you rest. Take my yoke upon you
and learn from me, for I am gentle and humble in heart,
and you will find rest for your souls."
(Matthew 11:28–29)

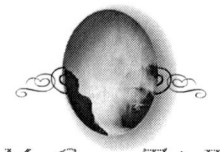

Help Me Carry This Weight

Help me carry this weight, Jesus,
for it is too heavy for me to bear.
I feel surrounded by the enemy, Jesus,
like Daniel in the lions' lair.

I call upon Your holy name, Jesus;
please deliver me from my foe.
I cry out for Your mercy, Jesus;
comfort me in this pain and woe.

Cleanse me with Your blood, Jesus,
from wallowing in this mire.
Make me holy and strong, Jesus,
as You refine me through this fire.

I seek Your presence and peace, Jesus,
as I bring all of my burdens to You.
Without You I am frail and weak, Jesus,
may Your Holy Spirit, my spirit, renew.

Help me carry this weight, Jesus,
for on You alone I truly depend.
Jesus, You are my Lord and Master,
my Savior, Redeemer, and Friend.

Anna Beth Fore

Then Jesus said to his disciples,
"If anyone would come after me, he must deny
himself and take up his cross and follow me.
For whoever wants to save his life will lose it,
but whoever loses his life for me will find it."
(Matthew 16:24–25)

Help Me Deny Myself

Help me deny myself, Lord,
and offer my life wholly to You.
Help me be a living sacrifice
and submit to You in all that I do.

Help me be like the apostles, Lord,
to leave everything and follow.
Help me give up wealth and family
and go where You want me to go.

Help me talk to you intimately, Lord,
as Jesus prayed at Gethsemane.
And help me to submit to Your will,
to live the life You designed for me.

Help me remember the cross, Lord,
and Your sacrifice for all mankind.
Help me remember Your promise
that all of us who seek will find.

Help me remember Your gift, Lord—
Your Holy Spirit is my guarantee,
clothed with a heavenly dwelling,
I'll live with You for eternity.

Help me deny myself, Lord,
and offer my life wholly to You.
Help me be a living sacrifice
and submit to You in all that I do.

Anna Beth Fore

Be kind and compassionate
to one another, forgiving each other,
just as in Christ God forgave you.
(Ephesians 4:32)

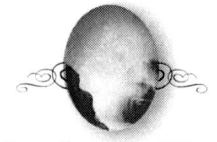

Give Me a Spirit of Forgiveness

Give me a spirit of forgiveness, Lord,
when others speak ugly words to me,
and when people stab me in the back,
or seek to harm me in ways I do not see.

Give me a spirit of forgiveness, Lord,
when others withhold their love from me,
and they are disappointed and resentful
because I am not who they want me to be.

Give me a spirit of forgiveness, Lord,
when others discourage and put me down.
Remind me that I am a child of the King
who is worthy of Your crown.

Give me a spirit of forgiveness, Lord,
when others violate or threaten me.
Though my body may be hurt or maimed,
Your Holy Spirit sets my spirit free.

Give me a spirit of forgiveness, Lord.
In Your presence, humble me and abase.
Help me be kind and overlook others' faults
so that others can witness Your grace.

Give me a spirit of forgiveness, Lord,
regardless of what others may do.
Forgive me, Lord, as I forgive others;
make me holy, and my heart daily renew.

Anna Beth Fore

"I desire to do your will, O my God;
your law is within my heart." I proclaim
righteousness in the great assembly; I do not
seal my lips, as you know, O Lord.
I do not hide your righteousness in my heart;
I speak of your faithfulness and salvation.
I do not conceal your love and your truth
from the great assembly.
(Psalm 40:8–10)

My Spiritual Desires

I want to lay down my idols, Lord,
and sacrifice my life to Thee.
I want to give up my fleshly desires
that tempt and encumber me.

I want You to change me, Lord,
and to rid me of self and pride.
I want You to cleanse my heart
and sanctify me deep inside.

I want to be Your servant, Lord,
and to be Your hands and feet.
I want to be transformed and refined,
after I'm sifted like chaff from wheat.

I want to reflect Jesus, Lord,
so that others will see His face.
I want to be loving and forgiving
so that others will know His grace.

I want to live a worthy life, Lord,
giving honor and praise to my King.
I want to live the abundant life
that following You will bring.

I want to stand in Your presence, Lord,
and hear Your words, "Well done."
I want to sing and dance in heaven
when the final victory is won!

Anna Beth Fore

7

Hope

And hope does not disappoint us,
because God has poured out his love
into our hearts by the Holy Spirit,
whom he has given us.
(Romans 5:5)

Hope Is Eternal

Where do you go when your heart is breaking?
Where do you go when your body is aching?
Where do you go when you're filled with despair?
Where do you go when no one seems to care?

God, You are our only refuge in the storms of life.
You give us strength in times of trouble and strife.
Your gifts of grace and mercy are new each day,
and when we trust in You, You provide a way.

Our faith in Jesus Christ, Your sacrificial Son,
gives us hope in eternal life when this race is run.
Hope is a gift that gives us comfort and peace,
and from this world's suffering, it gives us release.

Trials and suffering should be our heart's desire,
for You are faithful and refine us through the fire.
During these struggles, we learn to trust and obey.
We learn to be still and listen to what You have to say.

The cleansing blood of Jesus makes us holy and pure,
and as heirs of Jesus Christ, our salvation is secure.
Jesus is our Savior, our Redeemer, and Friend;
with Him hope is eternal, without beginning or end!

Anna Beth Fore

In him was life, and that life was the
light of men. The light shines in the darkness,
but the darkness has not understood it.
There came a man who was sent from God;
his name was John. He came as a witness to
testify concerning that light, so that through him
all men might believe. He himself was not the
light; he came only as a witness to the light.
The true light that gives light to every man was
coming into the world. He was in the world,
and though the world was made through him,
the world did not recognize him.
(John 1:4–10)

Lighthouses

Lighthouses stand tall and stalwart
on cliffs and shores of the ocean.
They are steady beacons of light in the dark
to wanderers on the sea in motion.

The foghorn blows its warning call
to sailors adrift at sea.
And guides them back to the familiar shore—
a safe haven for them to be.

Lighthouses provide guidance and direction
for all who wander in the night.
They embody hope and a safe refuge
for those who will follow the Light.

Anna Beth Fore

Then the Lord answered Job
out of the storm. He said: "Who is this
that darkens my counsel with words
without knowledge? Brace yourself
like a man; I will question you,
and you shall answer me.
Where were you when I laid
the earth's foundation?
Tell me, if you understand."
(Job 38:1–4)

What If?

What if I had been born beautiful, famous, and wealthy?
Would I be happier than I am today?
What if I had perfect parents with a perfect marriage?
Would I be perfect in every thing I do and say?

What if life had been easier, without struggles and pain?
Would I be wiser, kinder, and stronger?
What if I had successfully realized all of my dreams?
Would this have satisfied my inner hunger?

What if I had succeeded at everything and never failed?
Would I be pompous, self-reliant, and full of pride?
Would I understand God's love, grace, and forgiveness?
Would I understand why Christ was crucified?

What if I were completely independent and self-sufficient?
Would I ever have the need to seek the Father's face?
What if I were religious, successful, and self-righteous?
Would I see the need for God's forgiveness and grace?

What if Jesus hadn't left heaven and come to live on earth?
Would He have been able to intercede for all men?
What if His prayers were answered and He hadn't died on the cross?
Would we have a Savior to save us from our sin?

What if Jehovah God didn't seek us with all of His heart?
Would we know that it is His truth that makes us free?
What if God didn't give us salvation with His assurance?
Would we have the hope of living with Him for all eternity?

Praise to Almighty God for His everlasting wisdom and mercy!

Anna Beth Fore

Praise be to the God and Father
of our Lord Jesus Christ, who has
blessed us in the heavenly realms
with every spiritual blessing in Christ.
(Ephesians 1:3)

Gifts from God

The greatest gifts that we can receive
are freely given when we believe.
The gift of love came to this earth
when Jesus was born of a virgin's birth.
The wise men were given the gift of joy
when they beheld Jesus, Mary's baby boy.
The gift of promise arrived with Emmanuel,
as angels rejoiced and to their knees fell.
The Prince of Peace gave us inner peace,
from fear and bondage, He gave us release.
The gift of forgiveness came when Jesus died
"Father, forgive them—" He lovingly cried.
Hope was given to Christians whom Christ did save
when He arose triumphant from the grave.
These are the greatest gifts that we can receive;
they are freely given when we truly believe.

Anna Beth Fore

For there is one God
and one mediator between
God and men, the man
Christ Jesus, who gave
himself as a ransom
for all men—the testimony
given in its proper time.
(1 Timothy 2:5–6)

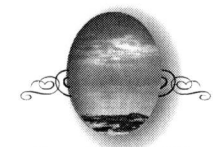

The Bridge to Heaven

The Garden of Eden was a perfect place
where You, God, and man were united as one,
until Adam and Eve sinned and brought disgrace
on You, the Holy Father, Spirit, and Son.

Man and woman chose the disobedient path
when the serpent tempted them to disobey,
and each was punished according to Your wrath
when they chose the serpent's way.

You loved man and paved the way for his redemption,
but this required a perfect blood sacrifice for sin,
which could only be offered by Jesus, Your Son,
who was the only bridge between You and men.

The blood of Jesus can cleanse all mankind
to everyone who will believe, trust, and obey.
And all who sincerely seek Jesus will find
that He is the truth, the light, and the living way.

When Jesus left earth and returned to heaven,
He left the gift of His Holy Spirit behind.
He comforts us and guides us from within
and teaches us to be loving, gentle, and kind.

Jesus bridged the gap and His truth made man free
when He was crucified on Calvary for us all,
and He assures us of a home with Him for eternity,
for everyone who believes and follows His call.

Anna Beth Fore

You are the light of the world.
A city on a hill cannot be hidden.
Neither do people light a lamp
and put it under a bowl. Instead
they put it on its stand, and it gives
light to everyone in the house.
In the same way, let your light
shine before men, that they may see
your good deeds and praise
your Father in heaven.
(Matthew 5:14-16)

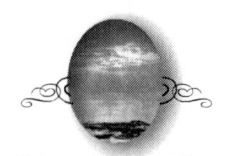

Keep Your Lamp Burning

*Christians are the lamps of God that shine in the night
who reflect the radiance of God's glory in the form of light.
When man believes in God and calls upon His holy name,
God gives him His Holy Spirit and ignites his spirit's flame.
As long as man seeks God, his body is filled with light within,
but the Prince of Darkness tries to seduce him with sin.
The Christian must resupply the fuel and oil for his light
by focusing his eyes on things that are pure in God's sight.
God's word is a lamp to our feet and a light unto our way,
and God wants us to put our trust in Him, and His will obey.
God wants us to shine so that all may see His radiant face
and be drawn to His holy presence and to His amazing grace.
Let's keep our lamplight burning so that all the world may see
that it is no longer I that live, but Christ who lives in me.*

Anna Beth Fore

Like the appearance of a rainbow
in the clouds on a rainy day, so was the
radiance around him. This was the
appearance of the likeness of the glory
of the Lord. When I saw it, I fell
facedown, and I heard the voice of
one speaking.
(Ezekiel 1:28)

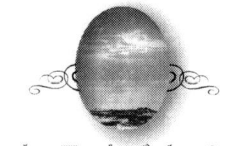

At the End of the Storm

At the end of every storm, Lord,
You give us a beautiful rainbow.
It's a sign to us of Your promise—
of Your faithfulness we can know.

Our days here have many troubles,
and we will stumble and fall.
But our faith and hope are in You, Lord,
for You are the Savior of us all.

When we're in the midst of the storm,
we often choose to ignore Your face.
But Your love endures forever,
and You reach out to us with Your grace.

When life's trials and tribulations
seem to overwhelm us with despair,
Your strength is present within us,
and You help us our burdens to bear.

Our hope is in You alone, Lord,
as we face struggles along the way.
And we can be filled with peace and joy
as You give us new mercies each day.

Anna Beth Fore

Remember him—before the silver cord is severed, or the golden bowl is broken; before the pitcher is shattered at the spring, or the wheel broken at the well, and the dust returns to the ground it came from, and the spirit returns to God who gave it."
(Ecclesiastes 12:6–7)

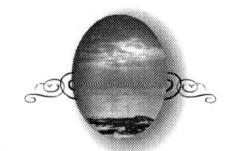

From Dust to Dust

From the dust of the earth
my body was made.
Into the dust of the earth
it will one day be laid.

My spirit dwells inside
this vessel of mortality,
but one day it will decay
and set my spirit free.

My spirit will soar to heaven
aloft on the angels' wings.
It will breathe songs of praise
as the heavenly host sings.

I will praise Almighty God
throughout all eternity,
as He reveals His radiant glory
for all the redeemed to see.

Come quickly, dear Lord,
and set my spirit free.
Take me home to heaven—
the place where I long to be.

Anna Beth Fore

Your kingdom is an everlasting kingdom,
and your dominion endures through all
generations. The Lord is faithful to all
his promises and loving toward all
he has made.
(Psalm 145:13)

Thank You for Your Promises, Lord

Thank You for Your promises, Lord,
that sustain me with hope and peace.
I know someday I will have no sorrows,
and all conflict and wars will cease.

Thank You for Your promises, Lord,
that there will be no more sadness or tears.
I know that if I believe and trust in You,
I'll no longer be enslaved to my fears.

Thank You for Your promises, Lord,
that You will give me a new name.
I know that Your Spirit is working in me
so that my life won't be the same.

Thank You for Your promises, Lord,
that you'll defeat the enemy.
I know that I'll be in Your kingdom
when You declare Your victory.

Thank You for Your promises, Lord,
that I'll stand before Your throne.
I know that I'll see Jesus there
and I'll never feel lost or alone.

Thank You for Your promises, Lord,
that I'll live with You for eternity.
I know that You've already prepared
a special, personalized room for me.

Thank You for Your promises, Lord,
that I'll walk heaven's streets of gold.
I know I'll forever be in awe of You
as Your radiant face I behold.

Anna Beth Fore

For I am already being poured out
like a drink offering, and the time
has come for my departure. I have fought
the good fight, I have finished the race,
I have kept the faith. Now there is in
store for me the crown of righteousness,
which the Lord, the righteous Judge, will
award to me on that day—and not only
to me, but also to all who have longed
for his appearing.
(2 Timothy 4:6–8)

A Christian's Legacy

My name is not written on buildings.
My name is not written in lights.
But my name is clearly written
in the worthy Lamb's book of life.

My wealth is not stored in banks,
in real estate, in stock, or in bonds.
But my wealth is an imperishable inheritance
as an heir of the King of all Kings.

My power and strength can't compare
with kings, or rulers, or wealthy magnates.
By my strength and power are provided
by God's Holy Spirit living in me.

My earthly possessions and treasures
will one day rot and return to dust.
But my spiritual treasures will live forever
through my God whom I love and trust.

My physical body will die and decay
like a breath and a fleeting shadow.
But my spirit will live on for eternity
to give honor and praise to my King.

My memory will soon be forgotten
as this generation of friends and family depart.
But the seeds God has allowed me to sow in others
may grow for generations in other people's hearts.

My greatest accomplishment in this life
is believing, receiving, and obeying Almighty God.
May the legacy I leave behind
reflect the love and mercy of Jesus Christ.

Anna Beth Fore

The throne of God and of the Lamb
will be in the city, and his servants
will serve him. They will see his face,
and his name will be on their foreheads.
There will be no more night. They will not
need the light of a lamp or the light of the
sun, for the Lord God will give them light.
And they will reign for ever and ever.
(Revelation 22:3–5)

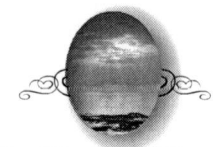

The Hope of Heaven

*My heart longs for beauty and peace, Lord,
in the presence of Your holy face.
My heart pants for happiness and joy
in my new home, Your heavenly place.*

*I envision a new heaven and earth
walking on streets paved with gold,
a new Jerusalem built with precious gems
where no one will ever grow old.*

*I see a place with no sun or moon,
for in heaven there is no day or night.
There will be no darkness in heaven,
for Your precious Lamb is the light.*

*I see the river of the water of life
flowing from Your throne crystal clear,
and I kneel in honor and thanksgiving
as the voices of angels I hear.*

*I desire to be in Your holy presence;
on Your radiant face I will gaze.
I long to sing with a glorious voice
and forever offer You songs of praise.*

*I beseech You to come quickly, Lord,
and from this sinful world set me free.
Please take me home to live with You
for heaven is where I long to be.*

Anna Beth Fore

From the fullness of his grace
we have all received one
blessing after another.
(John 1:16)

Flag TH74L
Betty James

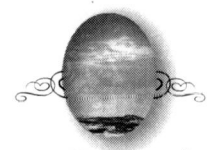

An Intimate Walk with You, Lord

*What a blessing it is to walk with You, Lord,
and to receive Your new mercies today—
to pause and ponder and be grateful to You
as I behold Your creation on display!*

*What a blessing it is to talk with You, Lord,
and to know that my prayers You will hear—
to share with You my most intimate thoughts
as You embrace and hold me near!*

*What a blessing it is to hear Your voice, Lord,
as You speak to me through Your Word—
to know Your love and Your will for my life
as my heart within me is stirred!*

*What a blessing it is to be led by You, Lord,
and to feel Your Spirit within me—
to know Your truth, Your love, and Your peace
as Your child whom You have set free!*

*What a blessing it is to know You chose me, Lord,
to be an heir of Jesus Christ, my King—
to live with You in heaven for eternity
as a new song to You I will sing!*

*What a blessing it is to know You live in me, Lord,
and You are my strength and my stay—
to serve You only and submit to Your will
as I walk in step with You along the way!*

Anna Beth Fore

May the God of hope fill you
with all joy and peace as you trust
in him, so that you may overflow
with hope by the power of
the Holy Spirit.
(Romans 15:13)

CPSIA information can be obtained at www.ICGtesting.com
Printed in the USA
LVOW13s0828210814

400035LV00001B/2/P